The Hospital

Focus: Information
Materials

PETER SLOAN &
SHERYL SLOAN

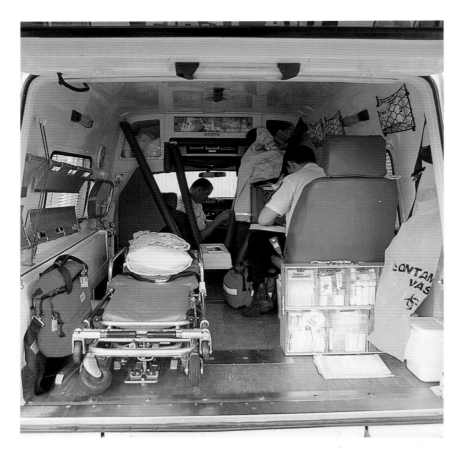

An ambulance is called
in an emergency. It takes
sick people to the hospital.
An ambulance is also used
when people must be
moved carefully.

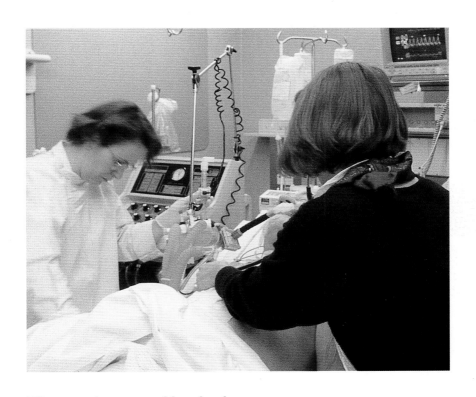

The hospital has an emergency room. People are taken to the emergency room when they have an accident. Sick people get help quickly in the emergency room.

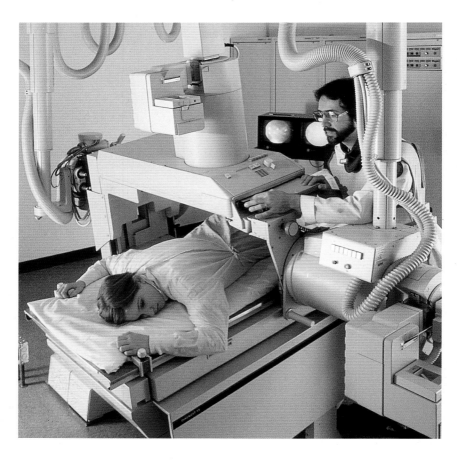

The hospital has an X-ray room. An X-ray machine is used to take photographs of the insides of a body. A person's skeleton can be seen in an X-ray.

4

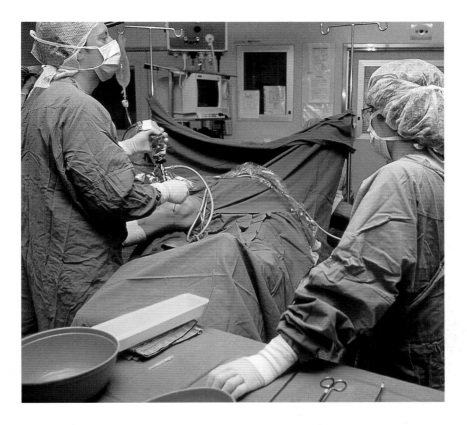

The hospital has an operating room. Doctors and nurses perform operations in the room. There are many instruments and machines in the operating room.

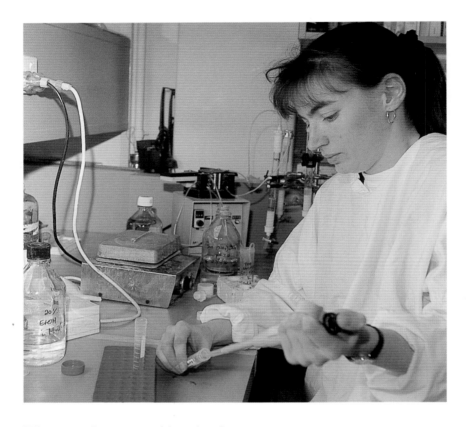

The hospital has a laboratory. Doctors and scientists do research and carry out tests in the laboratory. Doctors and scientists look for new ways to treat diseases.

The hospital has a pharmacy. A pharmacy is where the pharmacist gives medicine to sick people. Doctors tell their patients which medicines to buy from the pharmacy.

The hospital has a nursery.
Newborn babies are cared
for in the nursery. People
can see the babies
through a window.

Beginner 1
1. What **Has an Engine?**
2. All Kinds of Trucks
3. Making a Mask
4. What a Car Has
5. What Can Fly?
6. What Time Is It?
7. At the Library
8. At the Gas Station

Beginner 2
1. My Desk
2. My Milk Shake
3. In Space
4. Machines That Travel
5. Making Pancakes
6. The Space Shuttle
7. Making a Road
8. The Car That Stopped

Set 1
1. **Machines** in the Home
2. **Making** a Car
3. Tools at Home
4. Floating
5. The Class Newspaper
6. From Grass to Milk
7. My Boat
8. Growing Beans

Set 2
1. Using Machines
2. Electricity at Work
3. Parts of a Bike
4. Signs Everywhere
5. Sharing Time
6. Garbage Day
7. Baking a Cake
8. Front Loader

Set 3
1. Flying Machines
2. Rain
3. Trains
4. Using Fire
5. Wheels at Work
6. Big Machines
7. Making Lemonade
8. Fences and Walls

Set 4
1. Computers
2. Gasoline for the Car
3. Electric Motors
4. Making a Plane
5. Ships and Boats
6. Old and New Trains
7. Making a Tape
8. What If...?

Set 5
1. Water for You
2. Making Electricity
3. Making an Ooze Monster
4. Machines in the School
5. Build It Big
6. Instruments
7. The Hospital
8. Machines on the Farm

sundance
LITTLE BLUE
READERS

Little Blue Readers—the next generation in the
Sundance family of books for emergent readers.

Little Blue Readers begin at the emergent level for children
ready for nonfiction. These books feature stunning pho-
tography with engaging, informational text. In fact, they
are an early introduction to information reference books.
Little Blue Readers are graded and keyed at every level
to the following content strands:

Designing, Making and Appraising
Information
Materials
Systems

Teachers will find wide application for **Little Blue Readers**
in the daily science and social studies work in their classroom.
Children will enjoy the success of being able to read real "big
kids" information written at their own reading level.

ISBN 0-7608-3190-4

9 780760 831908

15070

GR Level – E
RR Level – 14